Bipolar Disorder

....

Understanding and Help
for Extreme Mood Swings

Edward T. Welch

New
Growth
Press
www.newgrowthpress.com

New Growth Press, Greensboro, NC 27404
Copyright © 2010 by Christian Counseling & Educational Foundation
All rights reserved. Published 2010.

Cover Design: faceoutstudio, Nate Salciccioli and Jeff Miller, www.faceoutstudio.com
Typesetting: Robin Black, www.blackbirdcreative.biz

ISBN-10: 1-935273-62-0
ISBN-13: 978-1-935273-62-2

Library of Congress Cataloging-in-Publication Data

Welch, Edward T., 1953-
    Bipolar disorder : understanding and help for extreme mood swings / Edward T. Welch.
        p. cm.
    Includes bibliographical references and index.
    ISBN-13: 978-1-935273-62-2
    ISBN-10: 1-935273-62-0
    1. Manic-depressive illness—Religious aspects—Christianity.
2. Manic-depressive persons—Pastoral counseling of. I. Title.
    RC516.W42 2010
    616.89′5—dc22

                                    2010020501

Printed in Canada
19 18 17 16 15 14 13 12   5 6 7 8 9

We all have mood swings. We can be a little gloomy one day, brighter the next. But if you are struggling with mania, your moods can be exaggerated and unrestrained, which makes life miserable for both you and the people you love.

These moods are not merely the normal ups and downs of life. For example, you may feel great and energetic. Most of us feel like that once in a while. But then the roof explodes: sleeplessness and racing thoughts are added to the mix and suddenly life becomes much more complicated. Or take optimism and self-confidence. There are times when you feel like you know what you're doing, and you feel good about it. But then self-confidence and optimism exceed their normal boundaries. Suddenly you find yourself at a blackjack table, vastly overestimating your luck. Next, with whatever money is left, you play a hunch in the stock market. You are so certain of success (although others have given their warnings) that you use your retirement money and max out your credit cards. You see, when you're feeling buoyant and "up," you believe you can do no wrong. And if something does go wrong, the problem doesn't register as a big deal. When your mood and energy level are at those higher extremes, you just can't imagine a bad outcome. Barriers to success do not exist. The experience can be such an infusion of confidence that you overlook any contrary opinion or circumstances that, when your mood is more restrained, would lead you to take a very different course of action.

These kinds of mood swings and accompanying behavior have come to be known as mania, manic-depression, or bipolar disorder.

How long does a manic episode last? An hour? A month? When will it return? Next month? Next spring? Next decade? Will you ever feel normal? What does it even mean to feel normal? Unpredictability is what you can count on.

Mania Is Unique to Each Person

The cycles in and out of mania are unique to each person. For some, the highs never become extreme and are noticeable only to family members. For others, mania is apparent to everyone.

If your mood swings were predictable you could prepare yourself and others for them. But with mania the swings aren't predictable. Without warning they can travel from low to high and back again. If you have the high, the low is almost inevitable. It's as if the body can't sustain the energetic highs, and its plea for rest over-shoots its goal and careens toward depression.

Focus, for now, on the mania. Here are some feelings you might experience during your high periods:

- Restless
- Energetic
- Garrulous; talkative
- A mind full of thoughts and plans
- Happy; up; funny; exhilarated
- Brimming with high self-esteem, without self-doubt
- Confused and out-of-control, especially when the mania won't stop

Subtract "restless" and "confused and out-of-control" from this list, and mania doesn't seem half bad. You may consider it a welcome change from the down times. And who couldn't use more energy? This is mania's subtle allure.

Mania Is Not Easy on Those Who Love You

Mania, however, is not a welcome change for you, especially when it turns into chaos, and it is certainly not a welcome change for your family and friends. Here's what others might see in you when you are manic:

- Impaired judgment
- Unwillingness to listen to advice
- Reckless, impulsive, risky behavior, especially with money or sex
- Inappropriate joking
- Incoherent speech
- Irritability
- Nonstop energy that keeps others awake (because they are wondering what impulsive decision you might make while everyone sleeps)
- Resolute self-centeredness

You are on an adventure; they are living a nightmare. They are never quite sure who will show up from day to day. Will you be the angry, irritable person? The person who won't get out of bed and sees misery everywhere? The person who looks like a caged animal and is preparing his escape to who knows where? It's exhausting for them.

Your family and friends welcome the normal times, if they come, but even those periods are tainted with fear because they are still haunted by memories of your last episode. It's possible that medication has reduced the extremes of your mania and others are grateful for this. But medication does not promise an end to the cycle.

Researchers once thought that mania and relationships just didn't mix, and not much could be done about it. That was before Scripture was brought to bear on this experience. Mania, although very challenging, will not stand in your way of knowing God, loving him, and loving others.

Mania Doesn't Listen Well

When you feel great, you usually don't seek help. This is the heart of the problem with mania. You don't solicit the advice of others. If you do, you don't heed it. You feel self-confident and on the cusp of important discoveries and major contributions. If anything, you believe that others should be seeking your advice. Be extra cautious about this.

The problem, of course, is not unique to mania. This is an everyday human problem for every person. When we feel something strongly we don't want to take no for an answer. The beloved goal becomes of critical importance. We *need* the thing we desire: sex, drugs, money, respect, love, morning coffee, a drive in the car as king of the road (without any moron getting in our way), a spouse who does what we want, a boss who respects all our contributions, or anything else we deem important. When we are calm—meaning that we don't feel too deeply about these desires—all is well. We listen. We might say no to them. But ratchet up our emotions and they are better called raw lusts. Suddenly, we must have what we want, and no one is going to stand in our way. It's no wonder that anger is so much a part of human life in general, and mania in particular. Anger comes when we want something and don't get what we want when we want it.

Scripture Speaks about Mania

Who's to say that another person's perspective is good and true? Other people don't know everything. Who has the authority to interpret reality? At this point, mania sends us directly to Scripture. Scripture has authority in our lives, which is another way to say that God has authority in our lives.

Scripture is ancient; mania modern. Scripture deals in the spiritual; mania in the physical. But if you are familiar with the Bible, you realize that it teaches us how to view *everything,* mania included. Scripture is God's communication to us: "All Scripture is God-breathed and is useful for teaching, rebuking, correcting and training in righteousness" (2 Timothy 3:16). It gives us wisdom to guide us in *all* situations. Whatever life brings—wealth, poverty, a medical disability, a psychiatric diagnosis—the Bible's wisdom is always rich and relevant to us.

With regard to mania, the Bible tells us that mania can't make you sin. Mania can't make you do things that Scripture prohibits (such as adultery), and it can't keep you from things that Scripture prescribes (such as love).

Mania *can* create a world of temptations. It can try to persuade you to trust your intuitive judgments rather than be suspicious of them. It can tempt you to believe that the best thing to do is empty all your accounts and play the lottery with a number you are certain will win. It can make wise judgment less natural for you because certain decisions *feel* so right. But it can't make you do anything that Scripture calls morally wrong.

This is, indeed, very good news! This simple teaching of Scripture is more hopeful and radical than it first appears. The popular understanding of mania is that it's a medical phenomenon. It's the result of unbalanced brain chemicals, and the treatment is to restore proper brain function with appropriate medication. The Bible doesn't argue with this theory; most likely there is a physiological contribution to mania. But the Bible goes deeper than psychiatric interpretations.

Psychiatric theories tend to see human beings as merely physical. Scripture portrays us as both physical and spiritual. Physically, we consist of brain, bone, muscles, and an amazing array of biochemicals. Spiritually, we are made in the image of God. We can know him and imitate him. We know the difference between right and wrong, and we are responsible for our moral decisions. Brain problems cannot erase these essential spiritual features of human nature.

What brain problems *can* do is cause our minds to race, leave us sleepless yet energetic, and make our thinking chaotic. But notice that these are not explicitly moral problems. They are neither commanded nor condemned in Scripture.

Brain problems *cannot* force us to ignore advice, live autonomously and impulsively, or move outside God-ordained sexual boundaries. They cannot cause us to follow our own desires at the expense of loving God and neighbor because these *are* either commanded or prohibited in Scripture.

When God's Word commands us to do something, such as love and listen, it speaks to us all. If those with chemical imbalances were exempt, we would all be exempt because none of us has a perfectly functioning brain.

Practical Strategies for Change

What we need is grace—God's help for us. We always need grace, but we especially need it when we would prefer to live without restraints and apart from any authority. The surprising feature of grace is God's favor on us, and he freely gives it. The only requirement for receiving grace is that we believe we are undeserving of it.

Acknowledge Your Need of God's Help

Start your battle with mania by telling God that you need help, though you know you don't deserve it. This might seem like a strange way to begin. Medication would be the obvious starting point, but you need God and his grace even more than medication.

Ask God for his grace to keep you from being led into wrong, sinful behavior. The Bible tells us, "No temptation has seized you except what is common to man. And God is faithful; he will not let you be tempted beyond what you can bear. But when you are tempted, he will also provide a way out so that you can stand up under it" (1 Corinthians 10:13). Nothing can keep you from living the way God intended you to live. Even during mania you can find a "way out."

If you are inclined to gloss over this step for change, please don't. Issues of authority, humility, and acknowledgment our neediness are critical in mania.

Distinguish Between Physical and Spiritual Problems

Keep in mind that there are differences between behaviors that come from an excited brain and those that reveal our relationship to God and his commands. They can be difficult to distinguish, but when you discover bipolar tendencies it is time to become a more careful student of your own life.

Here are some questions that can help you focus on matters of the heart:

- Did you consider others as more important than yourself? (Philippians 2:3)
- Were you quick to listen, slow to speak, and slow to become angry? (James 1:19)
- Did you seek counsel from other people for your decisions? (Proverbs 12:15)
- Did you seek God in what you did? (Proverbs 3:5–6)

Feeling a little guilty? Can you answer no to each one of these questions? If so, you should feel quite ordinary because honest answers to these questions reveal the heart issues of us all.

When we think about sin we usually think about condemnation. It is true that sin is against God, and it is serious. But let God's Word guide you in the way you think about this. The Bible teaches that conviction of sin means that God loves you and is graciously interrupting your turn away from him (John 16:8). It means you have the privilege of knowing the freedom and depths of God's forgiveness through Jesus Christ. Also, as soon as you describe your behavior as sin, you are saying that it can be changed. When you repent of your sins, God not only forgives you, he also gives you the power to change and learn how to live a brand-new life (Romans 6:1–14). So don't be discouraged.

The treatment for sin is confession. Start by confessing your sins to God. The Bible tells us, "If we confess our sins, he is faithful and just and will forgive us our sins and purify us from all unrighteousness" (1 John 1:9). Dare to believe that because of Jesus' death and resurrection you can actually be forgiven for every wrong you have done. Then take the next step of faith and confess your sins to those who were affected by them.

Confess Past Wrongs

You have already done the difficult part: you have humbled yourself before God and asked for his help, and you are discovering that confessing sin is not as bad as you thought it would be. When you confess, you will feel more human. Now, as an expression of your humility before the Lord, you can live humbly before other people also. This could mean that, if you have sinned against other people, you confess your sins to them with a humble attitude and a heart that is willing to listen.

Tell them you are beginning to see that you do selfish and hurtful things when you are manic, and ask for their forgiveness for particular things you remember. Then ask them what they saw and felt. What was your mania like for them?

You can't promise them that you will never experience another manic episode. But you can tell them that your goal is to learn to love and listen to others in all circumstances, including mania. This, no doubt, is enough to make you say, "Lord, help!"

Help Others Understand

Mania can be very confusing. When you look back on it, you're afraid you said and did many embarrassing things. If you ended up in a psychiatric ward, your embarrassment is coupled with shame. You'd prefer to avoid any discussion of it. Those who love you are also confused by it, and they also might want to avoid raising the issue. It's in this context that you need to put words on distressing events.

While you take responsibility for your moral choices, you also should describe the other changes you experienced—the racing and fragmented thoughts, the energy that made it hard for you to stop and relax. This will help you and your relationship with others. For yourself, the more you understand mania, the better you can manage it and even grow through it. For others, the more they understand the more helpful and patient they will be.

Your challenge is to find everyday words for experiences that are very difficult to put into words. If the words aren't coming, get some help. There are resources in every bookstore and on numerous Internet sites. Each story will be unique, and you won't find many stories that bring a radically biblical perspective to mania, but in those stories you will find words for yourself.

When you speak with family and friends, think of yourself as a visitor to a culture that knows nothing about your own. Think how challenging it would be to describe cars or faucets to people who have never seen them. This is what you are up against. It isn't easy, but if you care about these people, you will want to share something of your world with them, and you will work hard to find analogies and metaphors they understand. Here's one analogy you might find useful:

It is like a tachometer on a car. There is a middle
zone for rpm's when the car runs well. I feel
like I am either below that zone or way above it.
When I am going from one extreme to the other
I briefly notice, *Oh, this is what normal feels like.*
Then I zoom right by it.

Bless those you love by listening to their fears also.
Encourage them to speak openly with you. With their
help try to distinguish between behavior that is from
a manic brain and behavior that is spiritual—based in
your heart and your knowledge of God. Let them know
your plan. How are you getting help? What have you
learned from your previous manic episodes? Share that
with them. And don't let shame or embarrassment keep
you from asking for help. Let your pastor know what is
happening and invite him to help your family.

Be a Wisdom Expert

The spiritual problems exposed by mania—impulsive-
ness, unwillingness to seek or hear counsel, the tendency
to go down a path that has painful consequences—

are covered in the wisdom literature of Scripture. Your goal is to become an expert in this literature. Proverbs in the Old Testament and James in the New Testament should be among your best friends. You need to know them intimately.

Wisdom teaches us how to live the way God created us to live. It redefines what is truly natural to the human condition. As we would expect, it begins with God. Consider these verses: "The fear of the Lord is the beginning of knowledge" (Proverbs 1:7). "The Lord gives wisdom, and from his mouth come knowledge and understanding" (Proverbs 2:6).

Fear the Lord. If you experience manic cycles, you naturally want to bring the extremes into more normal limits, and medication is the only way you know to do that. But you can't overlook the obvious: life is about living for God in the ever-expanding kingdom of heaven, where Jesus Christ is King. To put it more personally, life is about knowing your Father so you can love him and become more like him. Don't let mania sidetrack you from your most important task. Since, in light of your manic cycles, you need wisdom now more than ever, the knowledge and fear of the Lord are essential.

What does fearing God look like? It looks like a life of humble submission to God. It means recognizing your constant dependence on him and your need for his guidance in everything. To grow in this, allow the Bible to stir up in you a desire for the fear of the Lord. Pray for it. Ask others to teach you about the true God who is to be honored and reverenced.

Seek counsel. You have heard this before, but you can quickly lose sight of it. The humility that comes from the fear of the Lord teaches us that we are creatures who need the counsel of others. Consider these verses:

> For lack of guidance a nation falls, but many advisers make victory sure. (Proverbs 11:14)
> The way of a fool seems right to him, but a wise man listens to advice. (Proverbs 12:15)
> Listen to advice and accept instruction, and in the end you will be wise. (Proverbs 19:20)

God has created us to live interdependently. When you are manic other people's advice can feel like someone throwing cold water on a wonderful, warm fire. This means you must start in this course of wisdom now. Do you know two or three wise people who will give you honest and helpful counsel? It may be hard to find people who are both spiritually mature and alert to the unique challenges of mania. Some people are intimidated by mania and prefer to involve an "expert"—someone who has helped others with mania.

If you can't immediately find a wise group of counselors, remember that wisdom is rooted in the fear of the Lord. So look for those who have a growing knowledge of Jesus Christ and a track record of spiritual faithfulness. Ask them for help, and expect there to be times when you will be able to offer *them* counsel and advice too. Get in the habit of following your advisors' counsel whenever at least two of them agree. This will become a profound protection for you, with or without mania.

Listen. You may have noticed that you talk more when you are moving into a manic phase. Sometimes you talk more, sometimes less. When you or someone else notices that you are talking more than usual, you will be wise to switch to listening mode. As you read Proverbs and James notice how often you find exhortations to listen. Your goal is to become an expert listener to God and other people. If you're listening to God, you will listen to others. If you listen to others, you are probably growing in listening to God.

Walk humbly with the Lord. Wisdom can be summarized as a lifestyle of walking humbly with God. We walk *with* him to grow in wisdom and please him by drawing close. We walk *humbly* because we're sinners who need the blood of Jesus to wash us so that we can experience the ongoing forgiveness of the Father and continue in relationship with him. And we walk humbly because it is natural to walk though life that way after we understand we're creatures who need the counsel of God and others.

Seeking Medical Help

Most people who experience extreme mania consult with a psychiatrist or qualified physician about psychiatric medication. There are new medications that appear regularly. Most of them are a form of Lithium or medications that have also been used to control seizures.

Should you try medication? Typically, you have nothing to lose and something to gain. At worst, you will have unwanted side effects, or the medication will be ineffective. At best, you will be less prone to the mood cycles or the more intense highs. Since you might actually enjoy mania (at least when it is not extreme), you might be reluctant to try medication. Talk to wise counselors and your family about this. You might decide to try medication as a way to better love others.

What You Can Expect

Mania is one kind of trial that we encounter in life. Like most trials, there is no guarantee that you will be thoroughly free of it before the future resurrection. Medication may help contain your moods; growth in godliness certainly will. Some who experience mania have found that growth in godly wisdom may limit the manic episodes and will *always* limit the damage done during them. But there is no sure way to erase the possibility of future episodes.

In the midst of uncertainty be assured that there is more going on than you can see. Your faith is being tested: will you turn to the Lord in your trials, or will you choose temporary independence? The Lord will use the challenges of life to mature you and make you become more like Jesus.

> Consider it pure joy, my brothers, whenever you
> face trials of many kinds, because you know that
> the testing of your faith develops perseverance.
> Perseverance must finish its work so that you
> may be mature and complete, not lacking
> anything. (James 1:2–4)